EVERYDAY LIFE

ROBERT HULL

FRANKLIN WATTS

A Division of Grolier Publishing

NEW YORK • LONDON • HONG KONG • SYDNEY
DANBURY, CONNECTICUT

4139200

Acknowledgements:
Cover images: AKG (bl and br); E.T Archive (t)

AKG London pp. 2-3, 15b (John Hios), 8t, 8b, 9b,
11b, 12, 16t, 17t, 19b, 21t, 22-23, 26l, 26r, 28b,
29b (Erich Lessing/Musée du Louvre, Paris), 9t (Erich
Lessing/Musée Vivenel, Compiegne), 13b (Erich
Lessing/Museum of Fine Arts, Boston), 14 (Erich
Lessing/Museo Nazionale Romano delle Terme), 15m
(Erich Lessing/National Museum of Archeology,
Naples), 19t, 20t, 28t (Erich Lessing/Kunsthistoriches
Museum, Vienna),25t (Berlin, SMPK,
Antikenmuseum) 20b; Ancient Art and Architecture
Collection pp. 5, 6, 6-7, 11t, 18, 25b, 27b; British
Museum, London pp. 14-15 (GR1920-12-21.1), 16b
(GR1910-6-15.4), 17b (806); E.T. Archive pp. 24t
(Archeological Museum, Dion, Greece), 24b
(Archeological Museum, Salonica, Greece), 27t
(Acropolis Archive Museum, Athens); Eye Ubiquitous
pp. 4 (Bob Gibbons), 23b (Anna Barry), 19m, 29t
(Julia Waterlow); Robert Harding pp. 13t, 22; Robert
Hull p. 23t; Rex Features p. 7.

Series editor: Rachel Cooke
Designer: White Design
Consultant: Dr Anne Millard
Picture research: Susan Mennell
Artwork: Peter Bull Associates

First published in 1999 by Franklin Watts

First American edition 1999
by Franklin Watts
A Division of Grolier Publishing
90 Sherman Turnpike
Danbury, CT 06816

Visit Franklin Watts on the Internet at:
http://publishing.grolier.com

ISBN 0-531-14538-7

A CIP catalog record for this book
is available from the library of Congress

GROLIER
P U B L I S H I N G
Copyright © Franklin
Watts 1999
Printed in Dubai U.A.E.

CONTENTS

THE GREEK LANDSCAPE

The home of the ancient Greeks is a land of islands, sea, mountains, and fast-flowing rivers. It is a land of brilliant light, with sun for 300 days a year. The Greeks farmed this land wherever they could. On the hills they looked after goats and sheep. And they sailed to and fro amongst the islands, fishing, trading, and fighting.

The ancient Greeks lived in a landscape of rocky coasts and high mountains.

MACEDONIA

PHRYGIA

• Larissa

• Dodona

Delphi • • Thebes

IONIA

Corinth • • Athens

Olympia • • Argos

Sparta •

CRETE

This map shows the important cities of ancient Greece. Places in *italic* were religious centres, the others city-states.

The City-States

By about 800 B.C. many Greeks were living in communities known as city-states, each a town with some land around it. Each city-state looked after its own affairs with its own coins, its own laws, and so on.

Athens was the biggest city in Greece. Inside its city-state territory, called Attica, lived about 250,000 people. Athens was a center of learning, and its new ideas and influence was felt throughout the Greek world. The military state of Sparta was Athens' only real rival.

Colonies

The Greeks also began setting up new communities—colonies—outside Greece. Some founded cities on the coast of what is now Turkey. Others went to Sicily and other parts of the Mediterranean.

Despite the separate states and colonies, the Greeks had many things in common. One Greek writer, Herodotus, described it in this way: "We are all Greek. We have the same language, the same gods and temples and way of life."

This map shows the areas of the Mediterranean colonized by the ancient Greeks.

History: This is a book about Greek history. The word "history" comes from a Greek word *istoria*, which means "discoveries."

■■■ LEGACY ■■■

We know about the ancient Greeks because of what they left behind: their temples and stadiums and the everyday things like vases and toys that archaeologists have dug up. The Greek legacy is more than this—we can still read their philosophers, poets, and historians, and share their legends and myths. Their plays are still performed in our theaters and many of the words they used have become part of our language.

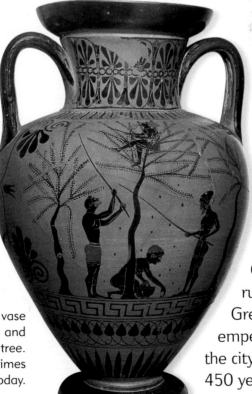

This ancient Greek vase shows men beating and shaking olives from a tree. Olives are still sometimes harvested like this today.

When Was Greece Ancient?

Greek history dates back far earlier than the city-states, with the Mycenaean civilization emerging about 1700 B.C. It continues through a time when Greece was controlled by rulers, like Alexander the Great and the Roman emperors. However, the time of the city-states, which lasted about 450 years, is the main focus of this book (around 800 to 350 B.C.)

CITIZERS

The ancient Greek city-state is sometimes called a citizen-state. This is because, by the 5th century B.C., citizens in some cities came together to make important decisions for the state, like whether to go to war or found a new colony.

"Our way of governing is a model to others. It is called democracy, because the majority manage its affairs, not just a few; ...when we pick someone for public office, what counts is his personal ability, not whether he belongs to a particular class..."

Pericles, an Athenian leader in 431 BC, as reported by the historian Thucydides.

These "ballots" were used by jury members to show if they judged someone innocent or guilty.

This is the platform in Athens where citizens stood to give speeches to the Assembly.

Who Was a Citizen?

Each city-state had its own rules about who was a citizen. Athenian citizenship was reserved for Athenian-born men and women who were not slaves or foreigners (which included other Greeks). Only men could vote and make laws. Occasionally, non-Athenians became citizens, but this was rare. In some other states, only wealthy people could be citizens, so the state was really ruled by very few people.

Politics: We get our word "politics" from the Greek word for city-state – *polis*.

Rule by the People

In Athens any male citizen over 20 could speak at the citizen meeting, called the Assembly. Then they voted, by holding up hands or sticks. The government was by "the people" not by others elected to represent them. In addition, men over 30 had to serve as jury-members in the law-courts. The Athenians called their government a democracy.

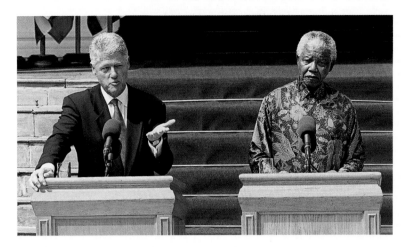

U.S. President Clinton and President Mandela of South Africa are both leaders of democratic governments.

■■■**LEGACY**■■■

Most countries today describe the way they are ruled as a democracy, based on the ideas that began in ancient Athens. There have been many developments since then. For example, rather than every single citizen being involved in every decision, citizens vote for people to represent them in parliament. And voting citizens are not just men, but women as well. It is also far easier for a foreigner to become a citizen.

Councils

Most city-states had a council that prepared laws for the Assembly to discuss. In Athens the 500-man council was made up of citizens over 30. Councillors only served for a year, and they were all chosen by lot. The council's role was to help the Assembly work better.

But in other states, the council really controlled the Assembly. In Sparta, Athens' main rival, and at times its enemy, the council was made up of men over 60, chosen for life; and they were under the influence of powerful officials and, strangely enough, two kings.

SLAVES AND NONCITIZENS

Slaves were part of Greek life. When Athens' population was about 250,000, at least 75,000 were slaves. The philosopher Aristotle said the slave was simply "a living tool." Only the very poor went without slaves, and very rich families might have 50 each.

A row of female slaves make bread.

Who Were Slaves?

Many slaves were servants—porter, nurse, tutor, goatherd, or bee-keeper—and, as such, part of the Greek household. Slaves even went with their owners to war. Other slaves worked in crafts and industry.

Slaves might be born and bred to slavery in a household. Free people might become slaves when they were captured in war, or kidnapped, or found when "exposed" as babies (see page 16). Very poor people might be forced to become slaves to clear their debts.

In Athens

Athenians believed that slaves should be well treated—one surprised visitor complained, "in Athens, it is not permitted to strike slaves." Even so, by law, slaves suspected of a crime or giving evidence at a trial were tortured. In the silver mines away from the city, slaves worked in narrow tunnels, on their hands and knees. Above ground they were often chained.

An old slave nurses a child. Figurines like this were often left as offerings at temple shrines.

In Sparta

In Sparta, there were fewer citizens and many more slaves. When Sparta conquered next-door Messenia, the Messenians became Spartan slaves. They lived in their own country, with their own possessions, but as subjects of Sparta—*helots*. They had to serve in the Spartan army and give up half their crops. "In Sparta a slave is really a slave," the saying went.

Prisoners captured by soldiers in war often became their slaves.

Other Noncitizens

Many non-Greeks were attracted to Greek cities, particularly Athens. These foreigners were called *metics*. They did not have citizen status but could own businesses and slaves themselves, and they sometimes became citizens. They included factory-owners, such as Lysias, who made shields, and Aspasia, a woman who trained young girls to entertain at men's dinner parties.

A worker feeds the flames of a pottery kiln. Potteries were often owned by *metics*.

HOUSE AND HOME

A Greek house faced in on itself. The outside walls were plain, with tiny windows, but the house came to life through the entranceway, beyond the dust and glare of the street, in a central open-air courtyard.

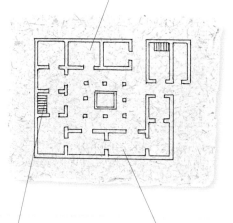

The "best" room, where men ate and drank.

Stairs to women's quarters and bedrooms.

The main work rooms, including kitchen.

Around the Courtyard

The main rooms opened onto the courtyard, which was designed so as not to be seen from the street and was usually south-facing. It generally had a veranda with a small colonnade and a family altar, and perhaps a shady fig tree. Even small houses had a courtyard; larger ones had two.

All the downstairs rooms opened on to the courtyard.

Roofs were covered with pottery tiles.

Windows were small and often shuttered.

Walls were stone-based with mud brick on top.

This is a reconstruction of a farmhouse. The plan above shows the layout of the rooms.

Well-off families had a slave-porter at the entrance.

In parts of Greece like this, where trees were scarce, timber was highly valued.

Furniture

There was not much furniture in Greek houses. They had boxes and chests for storing things, such as clothes, and low, three-legged tables on which to serve food. Ordinary houses had stools; richer people had couches and elegant chairs, with seats of leather or fiber cords.

Building Materials

Houses were usually erected on stone foundations and built of dry mud brick strengthened with timber. Wood and mud brick do not last, so there are few remains of private Greek houses. But some large farmhouses have been excavated, revealing pottery roof tiles and flagstones that probably paved the courtyard. Remains of smaller houses suggest very cramped living spaces, with some built directly into rocky hillsides.

Houses had wooden doors, balconies, and shutters to keep out the summer heat. In some areas wood was scarce and therefore valuable—during a war between Athens and Sparta, some people who fled the fighting even took their doors and shutters with them.

In this vase painting, a young woman is shown sitting on a wooden chair. It is unusual in a Greek vase painting that a subject looks directly at you.

FAMILY LIFE

The family was the center of Greek life. Their word for family—*oikos*—meant not just the people living in the house, but their land, buildings, slaves, animals, farm implements, graves, and so on. Each family had a male head, and when he died the family land was divided among his sons, who then started their own *oikos*.

Economy: Our word "economy," which we use to describe the managing of money, comes from the ancient Greek word *oikonomia*, meaning managing the house or family.

The tasks of spinning wool and weaving cloth were women's work.

A woman makes bread. In a richer household, she would probably have been a slave.

Family Work

Women managed the house and spent most of their time inside it. They had their own quarters, which were sometimes upstairs, and they were out of bounds to any man except a husband or close relative. There they made the family's clothing and the hangings and coverings for beds and couches. They also supervised the cooking and cleaning—or did it themselves—and looked after the children and the house slaves.

Out of the House

Women from poor families might work, perhaps in the market selling vegetables, but normally it was only if the family couldn't afford slaves that women left the house to fetch water or do the shopping. Women went to funerals and weddings, and public festivals, and they might pop out to borrow some salt or see the new baby. But mostly they stayed in.

THEIR OWN WORDS

"You won't allow us to leave the house, or even peep out of the door; And if ever you find that your wife is out, you bellow, you rage, and you roar... She may have been paying a neighborly call, on a woman who's just had a son."

A woman in *The Poet and the Women*, a play by Aristophanes, complains about being trapped at home.

Separate Lives

Men spent their working hours—if they worked—in the fields or workshops. Otherwise they could be at the *gymnasion* (gymnasium), the Assembly, the jury-court, or swapping news at the barbershop! Men were expected to be busy, but not usually at home. Sparta took this one step further. There, men ate all their meals in army barracks. Their role as soldiers was more important than that of family men.

Laundry was another task left exclusively to women.

WOMEN as WIVES

Women in ancient Greece were not independent. They were protected and controlled by a male guardian—first their father, then their husband and later still their son. They could not own property, except for clothes, jewels, and slaves, but in Sparta some women owned land. Even as citizens, they could not vote.

Marriage

Girls married young, often at 13 or 14. The husband was often older, 30 or more. Parents arranged the marriage. In the engagement ceremony, the woman's father "gave her away," transferring her from his family to her future husband's. The engagement was a business matter, agreeing on the size of the bride's dowry (the gift from her father). Sometimes, the bride did not meet her husband till the day of the wedding.

The Wedding

Before the wedding, the bride dedicated gifts, such as her childhood toys, to the goddess Artemis, protector of girls. On the day itself, the house of her parents was hung with garlands, and an animal sacrifice was made. After the marriage feast, as in the painted scene above, the couple drove to the groom's house, and the wedding guests followed. The bride's mother held a torch, taking fire from her daughter's old home to her new one.

A veiled bride burns incense as a sacrifice before her wedding.

An admiring Roman painted this picture of the poet Sappho 800 years after her death. But Greek men did not see women as their equals.

"The ability to think is not present in slaves; it does not work in women … the male is by nature superior."

The philosopher Aristotle

Once Women Were Married

Women could divorce men, but men often resisted, because they had to give back the dowry. Men could divorce women easily; the women were simply returned to their original families. A husband even had the legal right to kill a wife if he found her with a lover.

Within marriage, women ran the household, and some achieved fame, such as the poet Sappho. Women also served as priestesses in some temples, and there was once a woman warship captain, Artemisia.

The ruins of the temple of Apollo, god of prophecy, at Delphi. People came to Delphi to find out the future from the priestess, through whom Apollo spoke.

CHILDREN

Childhood in ancient Greece was full of toys and games, but before this a new baby had a frightening start to life.

This carving is of a grandmother and grandchild. Grandmothers helped their daughters raise their children.

A Dark Beginning

When a baby was born, the father inspected it to see if it was healthy. A baby who was at all deformed, or just very weak, could be "exposed"—left in a public place, either to die or be rescued, perhaps by a slave.

In Sparta, babies were the soldiers—or the mothers of soldiers—of the future. State officials decided whether a newborn baby was strong enough. Weaklings were tossed over a cliff. In the rest of Greece, the father decided. The baby who passed his fit-to-live test was accepted into the family, and given a name—often the first name of the father's parents.

In addition to those who were exposed, many Greek babies died naturally. Probably only about half of the children born to Greek families actually survived to the age of 18.

This child on a potty—waving a rattle and perhaps shouting, "Finished!"—is painted on a small wine jug.

A Normal Childhood

There is plenty of archaeological evidence to tell us about childhood games. In painting and sculpture, little ones play with rattles and dolls, doll-sized furniture and pots and pans, and little two-wheeled carts. Older children play with tops, kites, yo-yos, see-saws, and swings, or they bowl hoops or sit fishing.

A child plays on a "horse": a stick with a wheel at its end.

Greek children were told stories about heroes, gods, animals, ghosts, and so on. Their pets were tortoises, dogs, geese, and hens—but not cats. Dogs and goats in toy harnesses pulled their little carts.

Until they were about 6, boys and girls were brought up and taught together at home. After that, boys went off to school; girls did their learning at home.

Toy animals, like this terra-cotta goose with a boy rider, were popular with Greek children.

Pediatrician: We get the English word "pediatrician," a doctor who specializes in children's illnesses, from the Greek *paidion*, meaning "a child."

17

LEARNING AND SCHOOL

Greek laws stated that parents had to educate children, but city-states did not build state schools. Schools were private, for boys whose parents could afford them.

Future Citizens

Girls did not go to school but were educated at home and learned how to manage a household. Boys were trained to be citizens. By the 5th century B.C., Greek male citizens had to be able to read notices and write laws. They had to sing and dance at feasts and festivals. So boys learned how to read and write, how to dance, and how to play an instrument. They learned lots of poetry too, by heart, and math.

Some girls were taught to read, although they did not go to school.

■■■ LEGACY ■■■

The Greeks "imported" their alphabet in the 8th century, from the Phoenicians. They called the letters *Phoenikia*—"Phoenician things." Writing spread quickly, and by the 5th century male citizens were expected to read and write. The Romans later adapted the Greek alphabet for their written language, and this is the alphabet we use today. Our word alphabet comes from *alpha* and *beta*, the first two letters of the Greek alphabet.

A	a	N	n
B	b	Ξ	x
Γ	g	O	o
Δ	d	Π	p
E	e	P	r, rh
Z	z	Σ	s
H	e	T	t
Θ	th	Y	y, u
I	i	Φ	ph
K	c,k	X	ch
Λ	l	Ψ	ps
M	m	Ω	o

Grammar: Do you study grammar at school? Our word "grammar" comes from the Greek *gramma*, meaning "writing."

Training the Body

Boys were trained for the army, which was made up of citizens. They learned boxing, wrestling, running, and so on, at a *palaestra* with trained coaches. Boys exercised naked, which shocked foreigners.

Boys stayed at school until they were 15. Then they continued at a *gymnasion*, a large sports center with a running track. In Athens, young men of 18 spent two years doing military training there.

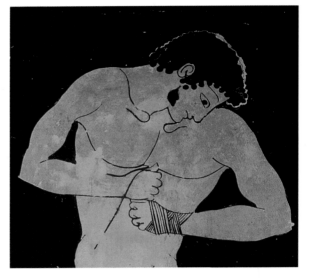

Boxing was always a popular sport in ancient Greece. This vase painting shows a man binding his hands before a fight.

We still train our bodies and run races. But trainers do not carry whips, as they often did in ancient Greece!

Gymnastics for the Mind

Because the *gymnasion* was where young men gathered, it was there that traveling teachers gave lectures on history, science, philosophy, math, and so on. Famous teachers set up colleges. Plato's Academy and Aristotle's Lyceum became the first "universities" in Europe.

In schools, boys wrote on a reusable wax tablet, carving letters with the thin end of a stylus. The broad end smoothed out any mistakes.

A Spartan Education

In Sparta, boys of 12 went to live in military barracks and lived there until they were 30. They slept in the open air and had to go barefoot. Part of their education was the "experience of going hungry." The aim was to produce brave soldiers, loyal to the state. Spartan girls had physical training too, so that as mothers they would produce strong children.

LEISURE TIME

With slaves and *metics* doing much of the everyday work in ancient Greece, citizens had plenty of leisure time.

A huntsman sets out with his dog on a leash.

Hunting

Hunting was a favorite rich man's pastime in early Greece. Men rode—without stirrups or saddle—to hunt hare, deer, and wild boar. They hunted on foot, too, with their dogs, and raced horses.

The Greeks had animals as pets; a character in a play says that he would like some pet pheasants, perhaps a heron. But the Greeks also enjoyed cockfights, between quails or partridges for instance. They even fed them garlic before a fight to "liven them up."

A replica of a gold drinking flask. It would have held wine.

Talking

Ancient Greeks loved to talk! After a few hours at the *gymnasion*, there would be news and gossip to exchange in public places around the city. Some of the philosopher Socrates' conversations were held at Simon the Cobbler's workshop. In the evening there was the drinking party—the *symposion*—in the men's dining room of private houses. Guests lay on couches, served by female slaves. The wine drinking came after the meal. There was discussion, poetry, and song. Everyone recited and sang. Drinking games were also popular.

THEIR OWN WORDS

In *The Wasps*, a comedy by Aristophanes, Procleon advised how to behave at a *symposion*. He has climbed onto a couch:

Just recline, gracefully. [Procleon lies flat on his back, knees in the air.] *Not like that! Straighten your knees, now pour yourself back into the cushions with a sinuous athletic grace.* [P. practices pouring himself into the cushions.] *Now you gaze round, up at the ceiling, admire the hanging rugs, the bronze ornaments…*

A guest at a *symposion* "pours himself back into the cushions."

These girls are playing knucklebones. They toss a bone and try to pick up others before catching it. It is like our game of jacks.

Women's Leisure

Wives did not attend *symposia*. Women do not seem to have had the leisure that men had. But they had plenty of opportunity to gossip and play games in the home. One sculpture shows girls playing knucklebones, a game like jacks, which involved throwing small animal bones in the air and catching them. In Sparta—as usual—things were different, and women were encouraged to exercise and move around as freely as men.

FARMING AND FOOD

Three main crops—cereals, olives, and grapes—gave the Greeks their three vital foods. Their basic food was bread from wheat and barley. Olive trees gave them olives for the table, and precious oil for cooking, lighting, washing, and even perfume. And grapes gave them their usual drink, wine.

Diet: Our word for what we eat, our "diet," comes from the Greek word *diaita*, which means "way of life."

In parts of Greece today, farming methods are similar to those in ancient times.

Growing Crops

The Greeks adapted wild olive trees and tended them in groves. They often grew corn between fruit trees – fig, apple, pomegranate, plum, and others. The smaller vines were free-standing, but others were propped on stakes or draped on trees. Greek farmers also grew crops like beans and lentils, celery, parsley, onions, leeks, and garlic.

Eating at Home

Greek meals usually had bread as the main item, with tasty side dishes like olives, leeks, cheese, and fish. Only a little meat was eaten, mainly pork and lamb. Rearing animals was expensive, so meat was mainly for festivals.

Unlike meat, fish could always be bought in the market. Writers talk of "fish-gluttons," including one who nearly died eating a whole 3-foot-long octopus!

Because Greece has such a long coastline, fishing has always been a part of Greek life.

This 7th-century B.C. figurine shows a farmer with his plough and team.

Farm Animals

The Greek countryside was full of animal sounds from donkeys, mules, cattle, pigs, horses, geese, hens, and —on the hillside—goats, sheep, and bees. Honey from hives was the Greek sweetener. From his animals, the Greek farmer had milk and cheeses (but no butter!), meat, and eggs. They also gave him transport and tons of manure.

Kalamata olives, much prized in ancient Greece, are sold in Athens today.

CRAFT AND INDUSTRY

The ancient Greeks had busy workshops and factories. They made ships, bricks, pots, beehives, drainpipes, coins, tables, jewelry, sports equipment, armaments, and many other things.

This gold wreath of ivy leaves shows the skill of the Greek goldsmiths.

A Center of Craft

Athens was the busiest city, full of craftsmen from all over the Greek world. An old law stated that citizens had to teach their sons a trade, but Athenian craftsmen were mostly *metics* and slaves. There were whole streets of small craft shops, and a Potters' Quarter—the *Kerameikos*. There was a mint in one corner of the *agora*, or marketplace, in Athens.

Athens had factories, too. The largest—Lysias' shield factory—employed 120 slaves. One factory making couches had 20 slave workers. But small workshops of four or five workers were more common. Smaller communities also had their own craftsmen, such as blacksmiths and carpenters.

This gold quiver for arrows belonged to Philip of Macedonia. Armor was made for show as well as for battle.

Workers mine clay for pottery. This tablet was a dedication left at a shrine near the potteries of Athens.

Rebuilding Athens

Greek cities were full of temples and public buildings, statues, and tombstones. But especially in the 5th century, when much of Athens was rebuilt after a war, stone carvers, sculptors, painters, carpenters, and others were in great demand, as were workers in bronze, when hollow bronze sculptures became fashionable. The bronzes were light to carry and didn't break.

Blacksmiths work at a furnace. One holds tongs, the other works the bellows.

The Raw Materials

All these trades depended on workers in mines, quarries, logging camps, and so on. Traces can still be found of the work of the men who produced the lead and silver needed to keep Greece prosperous. The fleet that defeated the Persians in a 5th-century war was paid for by a find of silver, in Laurion, south of Athens. Thousands of slaves and hundreds of free men worked the mines in dangerous conditions, carrying a chisel and an oil-lamp.

CLOTHES AND JEWELRY

Greek looms wove wool cloth in rectangular pieces. Greek women folded and pinned or sewed these squares in different ways to make the two main Greek garments—the *chiton* and *himation*.

This woman wears a *chiton*, the man a *himation*.

Chiton and *Himation*

The *chiton* was wrapped around the body and pinned in various ways at the shoulder. Women wore it to the ankle; men and children, and dancers, to the knee. The *himation* went over the *chiton* in cool weather.

Men often wore white, but brown for working in the fields or workshops. Spartan men wore flowing red cloaks. Saffron yellow was popular for women.

A woman, dressed in a *chiton*, admires herself in a mirror. She holds her jewelry box in the other hand.

Hats and Shoes

Normally most Greeks went bare-headed, but for traveling, or work, men had caps and hats. Fishermen and some craftsmen wore a conical cap, a *pilos*. Greek footwear was sandals—leather flip-flops—or soft boots reaching up the calf. Some women put cork in their shoes to be taller. Many people went barefoot in summer.

This woman is fastening on a sandal. Her hair is worn fashionably up and covered.

Hairstyles

Women usually wore their hair long and up, sometimes gathered into a net, scarf, or cap. They decorated it with pins or ribbons.

Female slaves wore their hair short. So did men, too, after about the 5th century B.C.. But earlier, in the 6th century B.C., men's hair was often long and bound in place with gold. In Sparta, men continued to grow their hair, as it was considered "the mark of a gentleman." Older men usually grew beards.

This boy's head was carved about 470 B.C. His hairstyle is one popular at the time.

THEIR OWN WORDS

Perhaps because Greek clothes didn't have pockets, the Greeks carried loose change in the mouth. One character in *The Wasps* is tricked in the market this way:

They hadn't got the change, and we were given a drachma between us, and we went to the fish-market to change it. But what he put into my mouth were three fish-scales—ugh!

The Wasps, Aristophanes

Makeup and Jewelry

Women used white lead (which was poisonous!) to keep the skin pale and alkanet root to redden the cheeks. Less respectable women wore eye makeup. Otherwise women wore plenty of scent and some jewelry— earrings, bracelets, and chains. Men wore rings, bangles, and armbands. Finally, to make sure everything looked right, they used mirrors of polished bronze or silver.

Hidden in the delicate work of this earring is a figure playing a lyre.

27

HEALTH

In many ways, Greeks lived healthy lives. They had a wonderful sunny climate and a diet that to us seems very sensible, and plenty of sport and exercise. But they did not have the same knowledge of medicine and hygiene that we have today.

A man scrapes himself clean with a strigil.

A young woman washes and scrubs her feet.

Life Spans

Greeks did not live as long as we do. Perhaps as many as 40 percent of Greeks were under 18 and as few as 5 percent over 60. Many teenagers had only one parent alive.

Hygiene: The Greeks had a goddess of health—Hygeia. From her name comes our word "hygiene."

Sanitation

Only a few houses had a private water supply. Water came mainly from public fountains or a well. Greeks washed in large pots, using sponges. They rubbed olive oil in the skin, scraped it off with a strigil, and rinsed off with water. There was no proper sewage disposal, only rubbish collection.

A bad harvest could cause famine. At times, in war especially, disease and plague struck: during a long struggle against Sparta, half the people of Athens died of the plague.

The doctor Hippocrates is sometimes called the Father of Medicine. He wrote a Doctors' Oath—the Hippocratic Oath—which was used for centuries in Western Europe. It sounds modern: *"I will use treatment to help the sick and never to cause harm... I will not give poison even though asked to do so... A doctor must not talk about what he discovers from a patient. Those things are holy secrets."* Doctors today are still not meant to reveal information about their patients—an idea learned from ancient Greece.

Perhaps because of diet and climate, Greeks today live longer than world averages.

Hippocrates studied at a medical school in Athens.

Medicine

The Greeks took a great interest in medicine. Writers such as Hippocrates offered advice that stressed diet, lifestyle, rest, and exercise.

Some doctors were priests of Asclepius, the god of healing. Greeks needing cures or advice had always gone to the god's "health resorts," with temples, priests, and hospitals. Others tried age-old magic methods and, occasionally, hypnosis.

In some cities, medical schools were set up. Surgeons and doctors from these schools sometimes worked for the state, for instance, with the army in war. They were well paid. The ancient Greeks may not have understood illness and disease as well as we do, but their ideas are the foundation for medical teaching and practice today.

GLOSSARY

agora: a large open space in the center of the town; a marketplace or square.

Aristophanes (c. 450–385 B.C.): the most famous Greek writer of comedies. He made fun of several well-known politicians in fierce anti-war plays. His plays are very funny and tell us a lot about Greek life.

Aristotle (384–322 B.C.): a famous philosopher and scientist. He observed and collected information very painstakingly, then classified it, and used it all to develop theories about many things.

Artemis: the goddess of the moon, hunting, and protector of young girls.

Asclepius: a god of healing, who was also supposed to be able to bring the dead to life. He was worshiped at an *asclepium*, a sanctuary where people went to be cured.

assembly: the group of male citizens who came together, or assembled, to make the decisions and laws that governed the state. The place where these meetings took place was also called the Assembly.

citizen: someone who really belonged to the city-state and had all the rights of citizens, unlike slaves and *metics*. In most states, to be a citizen, both your parents had to be citizens. Both men and women were citizens, but only men could vote in the Assembly. In politics, women were "second-class" citizens.

colonnade: a line of columns outside a covered-in walkway. In Greece, temples, marketplaces, and courtyards in the home might all have colonnades.

colony: a settlement of people who have left their own homes to live somewhere else. After about 800 B.C., Greek cities sent out many colonists, who were usually still citizens of the mother-state, or *metropolis*.

drachma: the unit in which Greek money is counted, both in ancient and modern Greece.

gymnasion: a kind of Greek sports center, where athletes trained and exercised. Some gymnasia were large and very well equipped; others were smaller. The gymnasion also became a place where teaching took place.

helot: a semi-slave from Messenia, who served the Spartans, giving them farm produce, manual labor, and military service.

TIME LINE

c. 1700 BC	Mycenaean civilization emerges.	c. 800	Greek trading posts in Syria and Egypt.	c. 700	Athens combines with towns of Attica to make one city-state.
c. 1200	Mycenaean palaces burned.	c. 800–500	Greeks settling all round Mediterranean and Black Sea.	534	First Athenian drama festival.
c. 1200–800	"Dark Age" in Greece. Knowledge of writing lost.	776	First all-Greece Olympic Games.	520	First naked winner in Olympics.
c. 1100	Greeks migrate to Asian coast of Mediterranean: Ionia.	c. 750–700	Homer composes his epic poems.	507	Athens becomes a democracy.
c. 1050	Iron in use for weapons and tools.	c. 750	Writing reintroduced to Greece. Also new heavy armor.	493	Silver found in Laurium, Attica.
c. 1000–750	Phoenicians travel and trade around Mediterranean.	c. 700	Stone first used for temples.	490	Greece invaded by Persia; Greek victory at Marathon.

Herodotus (c. 480–425 B.C.): sometimes called the first historian, Herodotus wrote about the wars between the Greeks and Persians that took place in his lifetime. He travelled all over the Greek world, collecting information about different peoples and customs.

Hippocrates (469–399 B.C.): the most famous Greek writer on medicine and healing. He looked for scientific explanations of illnesses at a time when many thought cures for disease came only from the gods.

Homer (c. 8th century B.C.): the blind poet who composed two great epic poems, *The Iliad* and *The Odyssey*, that were recited and performed in ancient Greece long after his death. They are still read today.

jury: in law, a group of people who decide at a trial whether someone is innocent or guilty of the crime he or she is charged with.

metic: a foreign resident in a Greek city-state, including Greeks from other states. Many *metics* worked as merchants and craftsmen.

mint: a factory where coins were made.

Mycenaean: describes the civilization that existed in Greece from around 1700 B.C. but seems to have collapsed about 500 years later. Many Greek stories and religious beliefs seem to have originated around this time.

oikos: the Greek family, including all the property in its possession.

palaestra: the sand wrestling ground that was a central feature of the gymnasion, although it could be found on its own.

philosopher: a word meaning "lover of wisdom." In schools and universities, we still study Greek philosophers, like Plato and Aristotle.

Phoenicians: a people from the eastern Mediterranean, who were very successful traders and travelers from about 1050 B.C. The Greeks borrowed their alphabet and adapted it for their language.

Plato (c. 428–348 B.C.): a Greek philosopher whose writings and ideas are a major foundation of philosophy as it is studied today.

Sappho (c. 600 B.C.): the most famous of several well-known Greek woman poets.

Socrates (c. 470–399 B.C.): a Greek philosopher whose ideas were very influential in developing Greek thinking and methods of discussion. He wrote nothing down. We know of him through his friend Plato.

symposion: the evening drinking party held for men in the men's dining room of private houses.

480	Athens burned by Persians; Greeks win at Salamis.	c. 445–426	Herodotus traveling and writing.	399	Socrates forced to take poison by the Athenian Assembly.
479	Greeks win at Platea; Persians go home.	431–404	Peloponnesian War between Athens and Sparta.	384	Birth of Aristotle.
478	Athens forms the Federation of Delos, so becoming an empire.	c. 430	Hippocrates working on Cos.	359-338	Philip II becomes King of Macedon and conquers the rest of Greece.
461	Pericles is a leader in Athens.	429	Death of Pericles. Plague in Athens.	336-323	His son, Alexander the Great, rules. His armies conquer large areas of Asia.
451	Pay for jury in law-courts begins.	425	Aristophanes' first anti-war play produced.	323	Death of Alexander.
447	Building of the Parthenon in Athens begins.	404	Athens surrenders to Sparta.		

INDEX